D1736777

RARE AND PRECIOUS METALS

SILVER

By Therese Shea

Gareth Stevens
Publishing

Please visit our website, www.garethstevens.com. For a free color catalog of all our high-quality books, call toll free 1-800-542-2595 or fax 1-877-542-2596.

Library of Congress Cataloging-in-Publication Data

Shea, Therese.
Silver / by Therese Shea.
  p. cm. — (Rare and precious metals)
Includes index.
ISBN 978-1-4824-0512-5 (pbk.)
ISBN 978-1-4824-0513-2 (6-pack)
ISBN 978-1-4824-0509-5 (library binding)
1. Silver — Juvenile literature. I. Shea, Therese. II. Title.
TN761.6 S54 2014
669.23—dc23

Published in 2014 by
Gareth Stevens Publishing
111 East 14th Street, Suite 349
New York, NY 10003

Copyright © 2014 Gareth Stevens Publishing

Designer: Nicholas Domiano
Editor: Therese Shea

Photo credits: Cover, p. 1 Fribus Ekaterina/Shutterstock.com; pp. 3–24 (inset graphic) Aleksandr Bryliaev/Shutterstock.com; pp. 3–24 (caption box) Hemera/Thinkstock.com; pp. 3–24 (text background), 17 iStockphoto/Thinkstock.com; p. 5 Scientifica/Visuals Unlimited/Getty Images; p. 7 Charles D Winters/Photo Researchers/Getty Images; p. 9 John Concalosi/Peter Arnold/Getty Images; p. 11 Chris Garrett/Stone/Getty images; p. 13 DEA/G.CIGOLINI/Getty Images; p. 15 Bloomberg/Getty Images; p. 19 Alison Gootee/FoodPix/Getty Images.

Printed in the United States of America

CPSIA compliance information: Batch #CW14GS: For further information contact Gareth Stevens, New York, New York at 1-800-542-2595.

Contents

Super Silver 4

Scarce Silver 6

In the Earth 8

Silver Mining 10

Ores 12

Refining Silver 14

Alloys 16

Why Polish Silver? 18

Recycling Silver 20

Glossary 22

For More Information 23

Index 24

Words in the glossary appear in **bold** type the first time they are used in the text.

Super Silver

Everyone knows something about the metal called silver. It shares its name and appearance with the color silver. Like other metals, silver can be shaped easily without breaking. It's also ductile, which means it can be pounded into thin layers or made into wire.

Silver wires and other silver parts are used in electronics because they **conduct** electricity well. Silver conducts heat, too. This useful metal is valuable for all these reasons and more.

METAL MANIA!

Silver was used as a form of money as far back as 800 BC.

Silver is a scarce metal. That means it isn't as common as other metals. That makes it valuable, too.

5

Scarce Silver

Silver—or at least things that look like silver—seem to be everywhere. You may be surprised to learn that there's not a lot of silver in the world compared to some other metals.

Silver, like all metals, is an element. That means it's pure. No other kind of matter is contained in it. Ninety-two elements occur naturally on Earth. In fact, many of them, including silver, make up Earth's **crust**. Silver is found in many locations around the world but only in small amounts.

METAL MANIA!

Some records say that silver was more valuable than gold in ancient Egypt!

Other metals include copper, iron, and gold. Metals are usually solid, shiny when polished, **malleable**, ductile, and good conductors.

7

In the Earth

Rocks that contain metals such as silver are called **ores**. Ores sometimes occur as "veins" in the earth. Veins form when melted rock from deep inside the planet rises up through cracks and hardens. The silver ore found in veins isn't usually pure. Instead, it's mixed in with other matter to form **minerals**. About 60 kinds of minerals contain silver.

A buildup of a mineral in Earth's crust is called a deposit. When a valuable deposit is discovered, the ore is dug up so useful elements can be removed.

METAL MANIA!

Galena is a lead ore that contains a small amount of silver.

This is silver in its native form. That means it's pure silver.

9

Silver Mining

Silver mining is an ancient practice. Greece's famed Laurium Mines were in operation earlier than 1000 BC. After the Europeans arrived in the Americas, most silver was mined there. Between 1500 and 1800, the countries now called Bolivia, Peru, and Mexico supplied over 85 percent of the world's silver.

In 1859, the Comstock **Lode** in Nevada became one of the most important mining discoveries in US history. More than half of the ore mined there was silver. Most silver mined today comes from Mexico.

METAL MANIA!

Nevada is still known as the "Silver State" today.

In search of silver, underground tunnels such as this are dug deep into the earth. Sometimes, huge machines dig large pits in the ground, too.

11

Ores

Silver is never the biggest part of an ore, but sometimes it's the most valuable part. Most ore that contains silver is mined for the elements lead, copper, or zinc as well.

The first step in removing silver and other elements from ore is crushing the ore into tiny pieces. The powder then goes through a process called flotation separation. The bits are added to water with **chemicals**. The metals rise to the surface in air bubbles and are collected.

METAL MANIA!

The silver at the Comstock Lode was mined from acanthite, an important ore containing silver and sulfur.

Tetrahedrite, shown here, is another important mineral in silver mining. It contains copper, iron, antimony, sulfur, and sometimes silver.

13

Refining Silver

There are many ways of separating silver from other elements. Producing a pure form of an element is called refining. Most silver is refined as a **byproduct** of copper refining.

During copper refining, electricity is used to separate the copper from other matter. This remaining matter, called the slime, is heated to a very high temperature in a process called smelting. Then, electricity and chemicals are used to separate the silver from remaining matter.

METAL MANIA!

When a lead ore is smelted with zinc, the zinc and silver attach and float to the surface.

Pure silver is shaped into bars called ingots.

15

Alloys

Have you ever heard of sterling silver? It's a silver alloy, which means it's a mixture of silver and at least one other kind of matter. Sterling silver is an alloy of silver and copper. Silver is a soft metal, so combining it with copper makes it less likely to bend.

Silver coins are usually an alloy of silver and copper or a silver-copper-nickel alloy. Silver alloys containing zinc or cadmium are used in **batteries** for jets!

METAL MANIA!

Electrum is an alloy of silver and gold that occurs in nature.

Sterling silver is 92.5 percent silver and 7.5 percent copper.

17

Why Polish Silver?

You've probably seen old silver objects that are a dull gray color. That happens when silver reacts with sulfur in the air. Silver and sulfur combine to form silver sulfide, which is a black color. When silver sulfide forms on a silver object, it's said to be tarnished.

The silver can be made shiny again. One way is to rub, or polish, the silver, removing the tarnished layer. The other way is to **reverse** the chemical reaction. The metal aluminum will draw sulfur from silver to itself!

METAL MANIA!

Movie screens were once called "silver screens" because they were made with silver.

There are special silver cleaners people can buy to polish their silver goods.

19

Recycling Silver

Because it's so scarce, an important source of silver is recycling. Batteries, mirrors, silverware, jewelry, coins, and electronics are some materials that can be recycled for silver. Much silver is used to make film for photography and movies as well. These things can be recycled, too.

Silver is worth more than just money. This precious metal's value increases with each new invention that needs it. Silver will remain an important part of our daily lives in many of the objects we depend on.

More Uses for Silver

fills dental cavities

collects the sun's power in solar cells

as a layer in DVDs and CDs

causes chemicals to react in certain ways

kills tiny harmful creatures such as bacteria in water

"seeds" clouds to make rain

coats some engine parts

coats some musical instruments

as a coating on windows that bounces back the sun's rays

21

Glossary

battery: a device that turns chemical energy into electricity

byproduct: something produced as a result of the making of something else

chemical: matter that can be mixed with other matter to cause changes

conduct: to carry

crust: the outer shell of Earth

lode: a deposit of ore

malleable: able to be shaped or bent without breaking

mineral: matter in the ground that forms rocks

ore: matter in the ground from which a valuable metal can be removed

reverse: to move in the opposite direction

For More Information

Books

Belval, Brian. *Silver*. New York, NY: Rosen Publishing Group, 2007.

Peterson, Christine. *Silver*. Minneapolis, MN: ABDO, 2013.

Tocci, Salvatore. *Silver*. New York, NY: Children's Press, 2005.

Websites

Silver
science.howstuffworks.com/silver-info.htm
Read about silver, its alloys, and its many uses.

Silver Element Facts
www.chemicool.com/elements/silver.html
Find out about silver and other cool elements.

Index

acanthite 12

alloys 16

batteries 16, 20

Bolivia 10

Comstock Lode 10, 12

conductor 4, 7

deposit 8

ductile 4, 7

electronics 4, 20

elements 6, 8, 12, 14

flotation separation 12

ingots 15

Laurium Mines 10

malleable 7

Mexico 10

minerals 8, 13

mining 10, 11, 12, 13

money 4, 16, 20

Nevada 10

ores 8, 10, 12, 14

Peru 10

recycling 20

refining 14

shiny 7, 18

sterling silver 16, 17

tarnish 18

tetrahedrite 13

uses 21

veins 8

wires 4